"**Clever, witty, and full of insights** on this complex phenomena we call leadership—this is how I would describe joyce's contribution to the application of leadership principles to everyday life. This book is written in her everyday voice, with compassion, humor, and just a bit of nudging to get the reader to think about doing things right, and doing the right thing!"

John "Jack" Azzaretto, PhD
Dean and Vice Chancellor Emeritus
University of California Riverside

"**WOW!!!** What a gift to have the opportunity to read your leadership book. I had the pleasure to read over the weekend . . . and ended the book with such great insight and ongoing guidance from my Executive Coach . . . You continue to amaze me . . ."

Linda Sumblin
Executive Director
CareerSource Okaloosa Walton

"**I must say it was a pleasure to read.** It was not like the standard leadership required reading, that I have been forced to read. Your book kept me laughing and thinking outside the box. What I liked the most were the real life stories, it was like I was reading a novel, instead of an instructional manual."

Judy King
Registered Nurse
Retired

"Instead of giving steps or processes to better leadership skills, *Why Are They Following Me?* takes the reader through a story and provides practical examples of how leadership plays out in real life. Having had the chance to sit down with Dr. gossom and hear many of these stories firsthand, it is clear that the life lessons learned by her are ones that we can all apply in our daily leadership roles. Dr. gossom, as outlined in this book, brilliantly forces you to ask the question, "Who am I?" and "Why are they following me" throughout your day-to-day life. **This book truly shows the reader how leadership is a lifestyle rather than a role or a position.**"

Jesse Westerhouse
President, Student Government Association
Auburn University

"Wow! From the beginning of the front cover all throughout, I saw joyce gillie, the person who follows lots of her mom's character but with the "touch" of her own qualities. Anyone who has the opportunity to open it up and dive in will grow, improve and develop to become a blessed leader. **The book is joyful!** The life-realness you put into your writing makes it pleasant to read."

Sherri Comer Williams
United States Navy, Retired

Why Are They Following Me?

Dr. joyce gillie gossom

Why Are They Following Me?

ISBN: 978–0–9890865–2–3

Best Gurl, inc.
PO Box 4235
Fort Walton Beach, FL 32549

To *Thelma,*
the best leader I've ever followed . . . con gratitud . . .

CONTENTS

Foreword xi
Introduction xv

"Why Are *They* Following Me?" 1
  Inclusion & Diversity 2
    Get A Bigger Tent
      (. . . You Need Everyone's Perspective) 4
    Put Yourself in My Shoes
      (. . . They Just Might Fit You!) 7
    I'll Take Personal Power
      (. . . Over Positional Power Every Time!) 9
    Find the Right People
      (. . . And Avoid "The Halo Effect") 11
    When People Show You Who They Are
      (. . . Believe Them the First Time!) 16
    Put Your Socks On
      (. . . Before Your Shoes!) 19
    It's Not About You
      (. . . It's About Them) 22

"Why Are They *Following* Me?" 25
  Vision & Strategy/Interpret & Translate 26
    I Can See Clearly Now
      (. . . From 40,000 Feet) 27
    Don't Fight
      (. . . Win!!) 33

Choose Your Battles
    (. . . And Your Strategy) 35
Sometimes Silence
    (. . . Is the Best Answer) 38
You Can't Win Them All
    (. . . But You Don't Have to be a Sore Loser, Either) . . 40
If You Always Do What You've Always Done
    (. . . You'll Always Get the Same Results!) 44

"Why Are They Following *Me?*" 49
    Character & Reputation 50
Leadership Can be Lonely
    (. . . So, You'd Better Like Yourself!) 53
The Upward Moving Spiral
    (. . . Learning to Lead With Wisdom) 56
Fearless Leadership
    (. . . Takes the Road Less Traveled) 63
The Harder My Head
    (. . . The More It Hurts!) 66
Push Your Chair In
    (. . . And Clean Up Your Own Mess!) 69
Is Anybody Following
    (. . . Because They Want To?) 74
Leadership Generosity
    (. . . And Authority) 79

Last Thoughts 84

ACKNOWLEDGEMENTS

To Melanie Baldwin for a rocking good title! To the Cowboy for the sometimes insane, adventures. To everyone who has ever followed me anywhere . . . I hope it matters that I've touched your life and that it means something. Thank you for allowing me to love and serve!

FOREWORD

Whether you are a new or seasoned leader, *Why Are They Following Me?* is a perfect book! You will want to read and re-read it during many points along your professional career. A written gift captured and shared by author Dr. joyce gillie gossom 's many years of successful leadership and professional wisdom.

Prior to the publication I considered myself privileged that Dr. gossom shared a draft for me to review. It is my pleasure to relate that *Why Are They Following Me?* is an outstanding book (easy and entertaining) that provides beneficial insight and ongoing reminders of skills needed for a great leader. As shared from Dr. gossom 's personal and professional experiences, she continues to amaze not only with her strength and leadership skills, but her vision for handling work place situations and personal events in a most proficient manner. It has been my honor to know joyce personally and professional for more than 15 years, not only as my executive mentor but also as my friend. Her background is far-reaching and impressive.

As joyce so correctly points out, a valuable but basic successful work philosophy is that, "It's Not About You (. . . It's About Them)." Five years ago, soon after I was selected as Executive Director of CareerSource, Okaloosa Walton, I sought joyce's counsel. I would often say to her, *"What have I done? Was I crazy to take this position?"* She very gently comforted me—assuring me not to move too fast and reminding me that it takes time in a new role.

She continued to steer me in the direction of success, by flying at 40,000 feet instead of staying in the "weeds," and lead the way for me in a confident manner. Reading *Why Are They Following Me?* reminded me of this basic leadership approach, which I still professionally apply.

Dr. gossom continually communicates the difference between personal power and positional power, which can be easily implemented in daily routines. She outlines the need for (and how to handle) stepping out of comfort zones to resolve or implement needed organizational or personnel changes in a professional and successful manner.

One of my favorite stories shared in the book, and one that brought a smile to me when reading, was how Dr. gossom related connecting processes to a spider web. I clearly remember many years ago when we first met and were in a meeting together, she shared her notes with me during the meeting. I thought her notes were not in a typical format, but rather were more like random comments with connecting lines. I could not image how they could make sense. Soon after my initial thoughts about the format of her notes, the meeting speaker asked if Dr. gossom would provide an overview of the session to the attendees. I had a quick thought along the lines of, " . . . *oh no!*" and wondered if Dr. gossom would be able to translate her scrambled words on the page. She immediately recapped the entire session using her spider web notes, as requested, in an extremely precise and accurate manner (no surprise). "*Hummm*," I thought, "*she is definitely onto a new note taking style, which could be beneficial.*" I immediately incorporated much of the spider web style into my note taking techniques, which now makes perfect sense!

But my favorite part of the book? I LOVE the title! Immediately when I read the title, *Why Are They Following Me?* My thought was, "*why not?*"–this is Dr. joyce gillie gossom. An individual I can personally attest has helped me through one of the most challenging, yet rewarding times of my professional career!

I hope that you find this book as helpful in your daily leadership role as it has been for me!

Linda Sumblin, Executive Director
CareerSource, Okaloosa Walton
December 2016

INTRODUCTION

I like to play with words and their definitions. It's fun to tear something apart to see how it works, then put it back together in a different way so that it's exactly what I need rather than what someone wants me to have. If you want to be technical, it's called analysis and synthesis. Or, just making it fit. I do it with words . . . machines . . . relationships . . . crafts . . . you name it. My friends and family know better than to ask me for a recipe because they know it's filled with things like, "Pour some milk. Shake a few flakes. Stir in a little powder" . . . drives them crazy!

So, of course I played with the words in the title of the book to see why they fit . . .

Why Are **They** Following Me? Because you take time to know them. Because they know you will protect them and make sure they feel included.

Why Are They **Following** Me? Because they want to go where you are going. Because they believe in your vision and that you'll get there.

Why Are They Following **Me**? Because they believe in you. You aren't perfect, but you are consistent . . . even when you don't know or mess up, you say so, and you talk about why you messed up.

Everywhere you look, there's an article or a book about leadership. We're obsessed with identifying the "Nine Traits of a Perfect Leader" or the "Essential Characteristics of a Great Leader" or even

"The Five Strategies for Becoming a Leader," but when I flip through the pages, the focus is usually on doing not being. During my life journey, I've learned a lot about being from many philosophies and religions.

> You have to choose which "wars" to fight and how to strategically fight them (Sun Tzu).

> Wealth doesn't come from having vast riches; it comes from contentment with yourself (The Koran).

> Greed will make a fool destroy him– or herself (The Buddhist Dhammapada).

> We can plan all we want, but the Lord's purpose prevails (The Bible).

> The definition of insanity is doing the same thing and expecting a different result (Einstein . . . and Nana).

> When you sacrifice your conscience for ambition it's like burning a picture because you want the ashes (Chinese Proverb).

It's not what you do, but who you are that matters.

It's a never–ending journey of self– and other–discovery; of learning who you are and becoming who you need to be.

It's choosing to take author M. Scott Peck's *Road Less Traveled*, where there are no road signs, mile markers, or speed limits. Heading in a direction that has something new to offer. Inspiring others to follow you on that road, to journey with you, to take a chance, and take a risk. If you are on that road, look behind you.

If the only ones following have to because of their position . . . Guess what?

If no one is following . . . Guess what?

If followers have no idea why they're behind you . . . Right!!

People will voluntarily follow leaders they trust, respect, like, or even love. They willingly follow leaders who have the balanced "qualities of wisdom, sincerity, humanity, courage and strictness . . ." (Sun Tzu, *The Art of War*).

To really become leaders, we need to step outside our comfort zone. We have to speak truth in the face of deception. To give unwanted advice. To call the ugly, ugly when everyone else calls it beautiful. Terminate a long–time employee for incompetence. Call out a powerful elected official for being a bully. Tell the boss's, boss's, boss that what she is doing is wrong without being afraid of the consequences. Telling the senior executive that you have options other than staying in a job and being harassed. Become comfortable with silence, solitude, and sincerity in the midst of noise, crowds, and flattery. Become lovers of light that pushes back darkness, forcing it into remote corners and shadows. Revealing realities that were hidden in the dimness. Light that reveals flaws, cracks, and tears. Light that illuminates. In those moments when there isn't time for a seven–step decision making process and there is pressure to conform or keep quiet, that's when who I am emerges.

When I served on the Fort Walton Beach City Council, I got to know Scott Paine, the Director of Leadership Development and Education at the Florida League of Cities. Scott had served as a Councilmember for Tampa, FL and as a faculty member at The University of Tampa before joining the League. A while back, he wrote a great description of leadership in a Florida League of Cities publication. "The best of leaders are as human as the rest. The difference is that the best of leaders have the courage to examine themselves, rather than simply to give in to the emotion and the moment. The best of leaders question themselves as well as others, and remain open to being changed by the answers they receive . . . For only when we know our true selves, only when we can be honest with ourselves and with others about why we do what we do, can we hope to win the [follower's] trust," (Scott Paine).

Building on Scott's description, "Leadership" by its very nature cannot be simply defined. In order to lead you have to provide what's necessary in a given situation with a given group of individuals to achieve the stated vision, goal, and/or objectives. The characteristics required range from motivational to directional and everything between to attain the desired end. When there are no willing followers, there is, by definition, no leadership. Therefore, leadership is far more dependent upon the actions and behaviors of the followers than on the "leader" him–or herself.

For me, leadership is about who you are as a person and how you behave toward others. After all, if you think about it, everyone is leading someone, right? So isn't it more about character, inclusion, and vision than position, power, and accomplishments? Isn't it about who is following me; and more importantly, why? These are the things I never stop grappling with. These are the questions I ask my mentors, my colleagues, and myself. Who am I as a leader? What do my followers need from me? How can I lead more effectively? These are some of my questions; maybe you have the same ones.

You can probably tell by now, this isn't going to be a ten–step book on becoming a leader. It's full of stories, random thoughts and half–sentences (smile). If you want five easy steps, put it down and pick another book. But if you're ready to look at yourself, start figuring out who you are and who is following you; who you are becoming, and why they're following you; then come with me on a journey of discovery . . . yours *and* mine.

"Why Are *They* Following Me?"

Inclusion & Diversity

Diversity is having a variety or range of different things. Inclusion means to make it a part of the rest, to not leave it out. That means we need to make room for everyone, not just people who are like you. Way too often for my comfort level, when people talk about "diversity" or "inclusion" they are only referring to a specific ethnic or cultural group . . . Diversity is so much more than that!

According to the 2014 "State of the Village Report" and the Office of International Programs at the University of Southern Maine, if the world were a village of only 100 people, there would be 60 Asians, 14 Africans, 12 Europeans, 8 people from Central and South America, Mexico and the Caribbean, 5 from the US and Canada, and 1 person from Australia or New Zealand.

The people of the village would have considerable difficulty communicating because 14 people would speak Mandarin, 8 people would speak Hindi/Urdu, 8 English, 7 Spanish, 4 Russian, and 4 Arabic. That accounts for less than half the villagers. The others speak (in descending order of frequency) Bengali, Portuguese, Indonesian, Japanese, German, French, and 200 other languages.

Also in the village there would be 33 Christians, 21 Muslims, 13 Hindus, 6 Buddhists, 1 Sikh, 1 Jewish, 11 who practice other religions, 11 who are non-religious, and 3 Atheists.

In our 100-person community 80 would live in substandard housing. There would be 67 adults living in the village; and half of them would be illiterate. 30 would always have enough to eat (half of those would be overweight), 50 would be malnourished, 19 would be undernourished, and 1 would be dying of starvation. 33 would not have access to clean, safe drinking water. 68 would breathe clean air and 32 would breathe polluted air. 12 would be disabled and 1 adult would have HIV/AIDS.

24 people would not have any electricity and of the 76 that do have electricity, most would use it only for light at night. In the village, there would be 42 radios, 24 televisions, 14 telephones, and 7 computers (some villagers would own more than one of each). 7 people would own an automobile (some of them more than one).

5 people would possess 32% of the entire village's wealth, and these would all be from the US and Canada. The poorest one-third of the people would receive only 3% of the income of the village.

50 would be male and 50 female. 89 would be heterosexual and 11 would be homosexual.

70 would be people of color and 30 would not.

18 couldn't speak or act according to their faith and conscience due to harassment, imprisonment, torture or death and 52 could. 20 live in fear of death by bombardment, armed attack, landmines, rape or kidnapping by armed groups; 80 do not.

Get A Bigger Tent
(. . . You Need Everyone's Perspective)

One morning, one of my neighbors woke up and went outside to sit on her back porch.

As she looked in her yard, she noticed something unusual sitting on the fence. She hurried inside and called her next-door neighbor.

"Bruce" said Abby, "Have you seen the 'M' someone left on our fence last night?" Bruce replied, "No, hold on while I go look." After a few minutes he said, "Abby, that's not an M, it's a W." "No," said Abby, "I'm sure it's an M. Look again." "I'm standing here looking at it," Bruce said. "Meet me at the fence." When Abby got to the fence, she asked Bruce why couldn't he see that there was an M on the fence and Bruce continually replied that it was not an M but a W. Pretty soon they started yelling at each other across the fence. They made so much noise that Harvey, the neighbor across the alley, came out to see what the problem was.

"What's going on out here?" said Harvey. "Bruce refuses to see that there is an M on our fence," said Abby.

"And she refuses to admit that it's not an M but a W," yelled Bruce.

Harvey looked at both of them in confusion. "But anyone can see that the thing on the fence is an E, so why are you two arguing about it?"

"What?" yelled Abby. "An E? That's not an E, it's an M!"

"I'm telling you, it's a W!" screamed Bruce.

"You're both wrong," said Harvey, "it's an E! An E, I tell you!"

Well the three of them made so much noise yelling and screaming at each other about M's, W's, and E's that they woke up grouchy old Lillian across the street.

Lillian came out of her house and walked over to the gate. She saw Abby and Bruce standing in the yard and Harvey standing in the alley.

"What's all this racket?" she asked. "You three made so much noise I called the police to report you for disturbing my peace."

"Abby says there's an M on the fence," yelled Bruce.

"Well, you keep insisting that it's a W!" Abby yelled back.

"And I keep telling both of them that it's an E," threw in Harvey, "but they won't listen!"

Grouchy old Lillian shook her head as she looked at the three people. "I'm glad I did call the police," she yelled. "I should have called the crazy house to lock all of you up. Any fool can see that the thing on the fence is a 3!"

My question to you is: What is the thing on the fence?

. . . It depends on where you're standing, of course! Mastering the art of leadership is essential in order to serve the greatest good. To do that, you need information. Not just what you already know and believe, but what others know and believe as well. You can only see your side of the fence but there are lots of other sides . . .

If you don't have people ahead of, behind, and around you who have different perspectives you'll always have a blind side because your tent isn't big enough for everyone, and all their perspectives, to fit!

During a visit to the US, Pope Francis told the joint members of Congress that the people of this continent should not be afraid of foreigners because they too were once foreign . . . That the people who are crossing the borders deserve being treated in accordance with the Golden Rule . . . "The yardstick we use for others will be the yardstick used against us over time," he concluded.

We are different in all of the ways that the people in our Village of 100 are different and then some. Even a short list reveals many ways we could and should include diversity in our hiring, promotion, and social interactions: age, gender, race/ethnicity, sexual orientation, religion, analytical/creative, political ideology, ability/disability, first generation graduate, veteran/military, socio-economic status, right/left-handedness, national and geographic origin . . . the list goes on endlessly.

At the same time, diversity without inclusion is a big fat waste of time. Why bother hiring or befriending diverse people, and then expect them to be just like you? Inclusion is the "closed parenthesis" of the equation. Don't make the assumption that just because I don't look like you, sound like you, come from your background, or worship like you, we don't have anything in common. If you take time to look for commonalities within the differences, you'll find that you can surround yourself with people who are both different from and similar to you. Do it when you make friends and especially when you make hiring decisions and your life and your organization will be richer, better off, and more productive. You'll have people following you who can see what you can't, have a different perspective or talent, and at the same time "get" your vision and want to go where you're going . . . commonalities within the external differences!

Put Yourself in My Shoes
(. . . They Just Might Fit You!)

Both Steven Covey, author of *The Seven Habits of Highly Effective People* and Karen Salmansohn, *The Bounce Back* Book author, have written about a critical element of leadership. Covey calls it, "Seek First to Understand," while Salmansohn calls it, "Think Like a Lion." Both convey the same principle that my Cherokee grandmother taught me, "Put yourself in their shoes."

Before you can lead, you must know who your followers are.

So simple. So rational. So practical. So hard!

I've watched hundreds of leaders. I've only followed a few. The ones I followed understood me. They took the time to know who I am, how I think, what I would and would not do.

The ones I followed knew, when they were told about something I had done, whether or not it was truth or exaggeration. They never bothered to even ask me about things they knew weren't true. They knew when a certain project came along, whether or not I was the best person to do it – regardless of my title or position in the organization. They also knew and recognized when I got restless or bored and needed to be stretched. The very small handful of individuals I willingly followed, learned to walk in my shoes, knew how I thought, and understood me. They didn't expect me to act like or be like everyone else. Or act like them. They also didn't expect anyone else to act like or be like me. I was chosen because I brought different abilities, culture, talents, needs, and skills to the table. All of their followers knew that they were valuable and valued. I would have followed them anywhere. And I did . . .

7

When I'm dealing with a challenge, I don't want to only be surrounded by people who can do what I can already do; I want to be surrounded by people who can do what I can't. I want to know someone will be able to pick out what I miss or overlook. I want to be able to call forward that person who has a linear thought process when we need to come up with a linear sequence of activities from the ideas we have brainstormed. That's one of my weaknesses. Why on earth would I want to be surrounded by people who have a spatial thought process like I do? [Think of a spider web . . . that's how my brain works . . . and everything is connected!]

You can tell so much about the most senior-level person in an organization by looking at his key hires. Especially the people who report directly to him. If they all look, sound, think, see, and act like him . . . it won't be long before the organization gets blindsided or finds itself at a dead end. That's the first thing I look at when I'm asked to work with a person as coach or with the organization as consultant. It's amazing that it's usually the last thing most people consider – if they even do. Is it uncomfortable to have people with different ideas, ways of doing and being? You bet it is!! That's why I need them (laughing). They keep me sharp and focused. They show me what I've overlooked.

I'll Take Personal Power
(. . . Over Positional Power Every Time!)

Being a leader isn't about doing a job, having a title, or holding a position. True leaders have "personal power." My mother always emphasized the importance of personal power over positional power. "People follow 'personal power' because of who the person is, and because they use their power sparingly. They follow 'positional power' because they have to," she would say. If you define power as the ability to convince others that it's in their best interest to do what you want them to do, think about how positional power and personal power each make that happen very differently!

Positional power earns compliance because of what you do, your title, your place in the hierarchy. *Personal power* earns commitment because of who you are. Sun Tzu wrote that commitment wins wars and compliance does not.

How often have you watched a woman play the, "Do you know who I am?" game with the person who answers the phone or greets her as she comes into an office or building?

I was standing in line at the check-in counter at a major airport listening to the man in front of me berate and belittle the attendant behind the counter. It was obvious that something had either happened to his ticket or that he wanted to change something. I could also tell that the airline attendant was doing her best to be accommodating, but that she wasn't able to do exactly what the traveler wanted. I listened with a small frown as the traveler continued to be rude and uncivil. Finally, he was finished and stepped away from the counter. I looked at the attendant, who had remained calm and unruffled throughout the entire conversation. With a small smile, I stepped forward and said, "It's terrible you had to deal with that." Without missing a beat, the attendant grinned and replied, "Thank you, but it's okay. When he gets to where he's going, his bags won't." I was stunned.

Positional power . . . at its worst . . . or at its best?!?

Find the Right People
(. . . And Avoid "The Halo Effect")

You already know that smart leaders know the difference between personal and positional power. And they know which one they have.

Even smarter leaders identify brilliant, capable people who have none or few of her own weaknesses and are different; and then she hires and includes them. "Hire your weaknesses, not your strengths," said Founder/Creator of Spanx, Sara Blakely.

The most brilliant leader shares the vision with his new hires, and gets out of their way! One characteristic or trait also doesn't influence them over all others.

When you are hiring someone, during the interview you instinctively tend to focus on the ways he or she is "like" or "not like" you; you also tend to focus on things you "like" or "don't like" about him or her. Basically, you form an overall impression or "Halo" of them. That impression influences your feelings and thoughts about all other aspects of his or her character, abilities, strengths, and weaknesses. You focus on their strengths and minimize or overlook their weaknesses. You "see" or "don't see" personality over productivity, ability over inability and/or appearance over qualifications.

It can be just as dangerous when you are the one joining an organization. Blinded by the Halo Effect of being like others who work there or liking the product or service provided, you can overlook ethics in favor of culture. You can also focus on activities instead of accountability or recognition rather than salary.

It does occur. It either results in, or gets in the way of, diversity and inclusion. It must be managed in the face of reality to avoid bringing in new followers who will gradually either become a disappointing challenge to lead or who will gradually become disillusioned with the organization or your leadership. It must be managed to ensure you don't exclude the very one you need to move the organization forward simply because she isn't "like you."

So how do you hire followers who don't all have your weaknesses and are different from you or others already in the organization? Strategic Interviewing!

How many times have you gone to, or conducted, an interview, and the first question out of the gate is . . . "So, tell me about yourself?"

Aaaaaagggggghhhhh!!!

Okay, let's establish some ground rules. You already know the finalists are qualified technically for the job because human resource personnel have screened the resumes or applications. So don't spend time obsessing over technical qualifications.

Once you have a pool of 7-to-10 finalists from HR, have a group of followers from various departments and positions do phone interviews with each one and give you a list of their top three-to-five applicants. Make sure they understand the position and how it fits within the organization, what other positions the applicants would work with and how they will interact with you before they do the phone interviews.

Invite the finalists to visit. Have different followers give them tours, introduce them to others, and have a group interview with them.

You take each one to lunch (breakfast works also). Watch how they treat the wait staff in the restaurant. Ask them about their greatest failure . . . least favorite part of their current (or former) position . . . kind of people they find it easiest (or most difficult) to work with . . . the most important thing they gained from going to school (high school or college) . . . some of the interests and activities outside of work that he or she would like to mention. Ask them what they would like to know about you . . . the organization . . . the other followers.

Above all . . . listen more than you talk! You're trying to figure out if and where they fit within the organization.

When you do find and hire that man, give him the tools he needs, support for his authority, a clear understanding of the organization, your expectations, and the vision. Then, get out of the way and watch him build relationships that steer the organization's members in the direction you've been trying to get them to go for months, or even years. When you find and hire that woman, the worst thing you can do is to get in the way, invalidate, or undermine her efforts out of fear or insecurity. Don't worry, she has (or will) figure out the landmines, the troublemakers, the obstacles, and the issues. She has also figured out the assets, knowledge keepers, and cheerleaders. The best thing is that with some guidance and grooming from you, she will know exactly how to introduce the productive and usher out the unproductive.

Don't let the Halo get in the way, whomever you hire, and keep in mind that you hired them because they aren't "like" you.

As you can probably imagine, I've hired lots of people throughout my professional career. Practically none of them were "like" me. They've produced my best successes as a result. A few became lifelong protégés . . . the two who were the least like me, in several ways. One was hired when I was running my business, Whitt Management Consulting, in Birmingham AL; the other, hired later in my career as the Associate Dean at the University of West Florida-Emerald Coast Campuses. They were both outstanding. Both served as my Executive Assistants.

Geoffrey Lakings is one of the most analytical, observant and interpersonal individuals I've ever met. He implemented brilliant processes for responding to client requests, completely took over my schedule and routine activities (work and personal, since I was a single mom at the time), coordinated all of the other personnel and consultants, and generally made my life less complicated. Geoffrey analyzed needs and filled in what was missing so that I could focus on the projects at hand and on securing more business. He was what every entrepreneur needs.

Joanna Soria is one of the most intuitive and fearless individuals I know. She also instinctively can tell who is really committed to the vision and who isn't. What's more, when she was my Assistant, she told me what I needed to know about people and proposed projects before I made strategic errors . . . she was never wrong! Joanna had a nose for quality and improvement and would identify and take on projects that made things better. She let me know when to come down from 40,000 feet (where I like to be the most) because she could always tell when I needed to reassure followers or adjust our course through my presence and touch.

What did I do? I gave Geoffrey and Joanna what they needed, and then got out of their way! As a result, WMC inc doubled business income every year for five years . . . and UWF-EC grew from 900 to 1800 in student enrollment and diversified our staff population by 50% in three years . . . with much of the credit going to Geoffrey and Joanna.

When People Show You Who They Are
(. . . Believe Them the First Time!)

It's important to know what gives you satisfaction and a sense of fulfillment. To know who you are. It's just as important to recognize that there are different paths to fulfillment for other people and to recognize what they need . . . and to know whom they are. Most of the time, it's as simple as listening and being observant. Other times it's not making excuses for their actions or words. "He's having a bad day . . . She's just tired . . . He didn't really mean it . . . "

Most of us somewhere along the way, have heard of the Golden Rule . . . "Do unto others as you would have done unto you." I learned the Platinum Rule as well . . . "Do unto others as they want to be done unto."

If I love flowers, specifically naturally colored daisies or lilies and you love chocolate, that's fine. But, if for every birthday and special occasion you give me chocolate, how well are you really paying attention to me and what gives me satisfaction? If you give me flowers, but they are roses . . . Again, it's not that you're doing a bad thing; you're just doing it more for your own satisfaction than mine. If I'm one of your followers and the best acknowledgement of my success you could give me is time off to spend with a parent who lives out of town or at home with my partner or child, yet you always give me a monetary bonus, how well do you know me as your follower? More importantly, how well do you know who I really am and how long do you think I'll continue to follow you?

One of my best friends, Karen Rones, called me one day in a furious tirade. Everyone who knows Karen also knows when that

16

happens, to just sit back, put your feet up, and be prepared to listen while she tells you the entire story with all the details (laughing)!

The bottom line this time was that her friend "Isabel" had done yet another petty and hurtful thing to her and she just didn't understand how Isabel could have done so.

I listened to everything she said.

When she finished I replied, "Rones, that's no different from what she has always done."

"No," Karen insisted. "This was different. She had to know what she was doing and that it would hurt my feelings. There is no way she couldn't because we talked about it beforehand and then she did it anyway."

I waited.

"Rones, she has been showing you who she is for the last 20-years . . . you just haven't believed her so she keeps showing you . . . over and over again."

Silence.

Finally, "I hate it when you're right, gossom!!"

More silence.

"Okay. She does treat me that way all the time when what I need from her gets in the way of what she wants for herself," she continued. "I need to believe that she really isn't my friend and is just another co-worker after all." More silence, then a sigh. "Okay, I've got it and I'm done."

"Good," I responded. "I'm tired of seeing you hurt by someone who really isn't a friend and watching you make excuses for her behavior."

We shared a few laughs. Caught up on families and hung up.

People tell and show us who they are every day. We just have to hear and see them rather than assume they're just like us in terms of behavior, likes, and preferences. People show us who they really are, and what they like fairly early in a work or personal relationship. The good. The bad. The ugly. The problem is that we usually don't believe them the first time and either make allowances, excuses, or expect them to change!

They don't.

Put Your Socks On
(. . . Before Your Shoes!)

Every single person you will ever meet or have ever met is no better and no less than you are.

I learned that lesson the hard way.

When I was about 11 or 12, right in the middle of that horrible period when you aren't quite a teen but you don't want to be lumped in with the "babies," I brought a friend home from school for an overnight sleep over. After dumping our things in my room, we went to the kitchen for a snack. We made a small mess . . . not a big one, but you could tell someone had been in the kitchen. As I headed out of the kitchen and toward my bedroom, my friend said, "Don't we need to clean this up?" If only I had just said "yes" and gone back. Instead, in all my pre-adolescent brattiness, I said, "Don't worry about it. The maid will clean it up," and kept walking.

At this point, there are a few things you need to know. First, that was not the way I was raised to behave or treat people. Second, I had never, ever heard any of the wonderful women who took care of us called a "maid" by anyone in our family (but I did hear it on TV!). Third, and most important, I had no idea my mom was home from work.

I had taken about two steps when my shoulders were grabbed from behind and I was spun around so quickly it made me dizzy. Shaking my head, I looked straight into the eyes of my mother whose nose was an inch from mine. You know that "look" most mothers can call up on demand? Yeah. That's the one. She's giving me the look and talking so softly I know I'm going to die,

"Who. Do. You. Think. You. Are?" I opened my mouth, "Don't. You. Know. That. Without. Wonderful. People. Like. Mrs. 'A.' You. Couldn't. Have. The. Life. You. Do?" she interrupted me. I opened my mouth again, "Don't you ever let me hear you belittle anyone ever again in your life, do you understand me joyce karen gillie?" she cut me off. I tried one last time. "Can you put your shoes on before your socks?" she interrupted. This time I didn't even bother. "Well. Can you?" Not risking it, I just shook my head "no." "That's right," she whispered, moving even closer, her eyes almost slits in her face. "And as long as you are breathing on this earth (yep, she really did say stuff like that) and you have to put your socks on before your shoes, you better not ever forget that you are no better and no less than anyone else; so treat them accordingly." I frowned, "Huh?" "Unless someone can put their shoes on before their socks, they're just like you and you're just like them. You are no better than they are. They are no better than you are. Therefore, you should treat everyone, no matter who they are or what they do, like royalty . . . " There was a long pause as it sunk in. *Wait. What good is being in charge if I can't tell people what to do or ignore the ones who aren't important?* I thought.

Mommy wasn't finished. Straightening up, she moved around behind me, gave me a little push, and said in her normal voice, "Now, go apologize to Mrs. A and tell her how sorry you are." To my horror, both my girlfriend and our housekeeper were standing in the hallway looking at us. My face got hot and red, my hands clammy. *What if she tells everyone at school?* I thought, looking at my friend. Another push from Mommy. "Now." Completely embarrassed, I walked over to our housekeeper and held out my hand to shake hers. "I'm really sorry, Mrs. A," I said to her as tears began to fall. I thought about how she had taken care of me when I had chicken pox, mumps, and measles. How she would put little notes in my lunch bag. The way she would make me a special snack on my birthday. The way she kept our home spotless and smelling so good. I thought about all that and more. I was suddenly ashamed for the first time in my life. It was a hot, sick feeling. "I love you and I'm so sorry I said that about you. Please . . . " I couldn't continue.

Mrs. A pulled me into her arms, stroking my head. "Shhh, child. It's a hard lesson to learn, but one you'll never forget. Of course I forgive you." By now, I was sobbing. Embarrassed and ashamed, yet also relieved that I'd been able to apologize and really mean it. Even more relieved that she could forgive me. It is, in fact, a lesson I have *never* forgotten.

Through the years, I've learned pretty much all I need to know about a person by how they treat people who don't have the same status, money, or privilege they do. I've asked of myself and of those I've followed: Who are you as a leader? How would your followers answer that question? How would the person you follow answer? Like many, I've thought about the characteristics I need and where my flaws are. What characteristics am I missing? How and from whom can I learn what I need? Where are my strengths? How do I use them for the benefit of my followers?

Who I am and what I do when I think no one is watching is character. The problem is, someone is always watching, whether I'm aware or not. That is consistency. Do your followers always know where they're going? What kind of people are they; do they have a choice about following you? Are they helpless and relying on you to be consistent and dependable? What kind of person are you and do you treat everyone like royalty?

It's Not About You
(. . . It's About Them)

As a consultant, I've worked with lots of companies and organizations. Regardless of how large or small, government or private, education or labor . . . top-down initiatives pretty much never work. The employees or constituents just wait the leader out! As an employee told me once during a focus group, "I was here before he got here and I'll be here after he's gone." We were talking about why a strategic accountability initiative started by the CEO wasn't working (beside the fact that it wasn't specific to the responsibilities of departments and divisions and it was really time consuming). She was right. As I looked through the corporate history, I saw millions of dollars that had been spent on one top-down initiative after another in an effort to have "accountability, quality, teamwork, communication . . . " and all those other buzzwords. That money could have been much better spent and results realized if the CEO had asked employees to answer one question: What's next?

The people who follow you know what they're capable of doing. We just don't ask them often enough. If we did, we'd find out that they could do way more than we think they can. So, why don't we?

Find out what should be the next goal from those who will carry it out. Then, draw a vision of being there that they can hold on to. Give them a roadmap; let them know what obstacles they will encounter. Fly up to 40,000 feet and lead the way. The result will be better than anything you could sit in your office and come up with!

As an Executive Coach, I've used the illustration of riding a roller coaster to describe the first year to year and a half for new executives. I encourage them to picture the long climb up that first hill and to think of that as getting into the position. That moment you experience from just before the crest of the hill to just before the first drop is the honeymoon period. Racing down the first and highest hill is the discovery of the true circumstances in the organization . . . "What have I done? Was I crazy to take this position? How could he leave me with this mess?" Going around the first curve is realizing that someone has to go; they can't hold on and stay in the seat they are in now. The straightaway before the smaller hills makes you feel, "Okay. All righty now! I've got this." Then, you hit the four or five hills and valleys before the last straightaway and feel baffled again because you've already dealt with that and now you have to address it again, and again, and again! When you finally reach the straightaway and are pulling into the station, there's a big grin on your face; you're looking to see who jumped off, and who's ready for the next ride.

So, here is the advice I give new executives. Ride in the first car so your followers see that you're on the ride with them and aren't afraid of what's coming. Hold on to the safety bar. Yell when it's exhilarating. Close your eyes when it's scary. LOL when it's over.

Love your followers because you selected them. You chose them when you joined the organization. It doesn't matter if the "organization" is a family, friendship, project, or company.

Stop.

Let's be clear.

True leadership, like love, requires voluntarily laying aside your own sense of entitlement or privilege.

Let's be honest . . . we all have some form of privilege, even if it isn't comfortable to admit that we do. She is the CEO; they are the employees. He is the teacher; they are the students. She is the parent; they are the children. He is the athlete; they are the fans. She has a college degree; he doesn't.

Like love, it requires taking on misunderstanding, isolation, and sometimes ill-treatment for the benefit of those who follow.

No, it's not fair. But the price of leading never is.

I equate it with love because I believe the two are inseparable. To use the Ancient Greek terms, it's not phileo, where a mutual exchange in equal measures is required. Not eros either. It's agape, the kind of love that wants and finds the best for others. The kind that is committed to give what the other needs. The kind that requires strength of character, knowledge of self, and abiding belief in a greater cause.

Love in this sense is based on choice – not emotion. It is a deliberate act of goodness (what is best for the recipient) not some kind of vague 'treat everyone the same.' It's based on knowing the likes and dislikes, strengths and weaknesses, capabilities and needs, benefits and disadvantages of every single person who follows you. Love is including each person on the team, telling them what their purpose is so they know their role and why it matters.

"Why Are They *Following* Me?"

VISION & STRATEGY/INTERPRET & TRANSLATE

Vision is the ability to plan the future with imagination or wisdom in terms of what could be. Strategy is a plan of action to achieve overall aim. To interpret is to explain the meaning of information, words, or actions. Translate means to convert information, words, or actions from one form into another that the listener can understand and implement.

Some people have a great capacity for vision. They see what others don't. They believe what others can't. They know what others haven't figured out yet. They have the ability to get others to see, believe, and know what doesn't exist and what hasn't been conceived yet. It's the ability to persuade followers to realize, go after, and accomplish things that seem impossible and unimaginable. Others have a great capacity for strategy. They can figure out the most efficient way to get where they want you to go. They can anticipate obstacles and roadblocks while navigating around them without losing time, people, or resources. There are also those who can interpret and translate the vision or the strategy and make it understandable by those who do the implementing. Making sure that no one is left out, unsure, or uncertain about what he should do or where she is going.

I Can See Clearly Now
(. . . From 40,000 Feet)

For me, there are two kinds of leaders, those who envision and strategize, and those who interpret and translate. A lot has been written and discussed about the difference between the two. Some call them leading and managing. Here's what I've learned.

You need both. At different times, for different reasons, to get where you're going. Let's use distance and airplanes as an example. Right, here goes my spatial thinking again . . . (laughing)!

The distance we can see in an airplane on the ground equals about 1¼ miles times the square root of the eye height (above the ground) in feet.

What does *that* have to do with leadership? Hold on . . . I'm getting there!

At ground level, the horizon appears between 2½ to 3 miles away. For the sake of the example, let's say that being able to see the horizon three miles out is the equivalent of one day. So, in terms of "vision," you can see, anticipate, and plan for just that day when you're on the ground.

If you go up about 9 or 10 stories, (about 100 feet), you can see about 12 miles away or about 4 days-to 1 week.

When the plane gets up to 3,000 feet, you can see about 67 miles into the distance . . . about 1 month, to continue our example.

At 16,000 feet, you can see about 156 miles . . . or 2 months.

At 40,000 feet, you can see for 246 miles around you . . . 3 months.

What's the point? At some point, you have to fly at 40,000 feet in order to be effective. You can't stay on the ground, able to see no further than those who are following you. That's a recipe for going over the cliff.

A visionary and strategic leader rises up to 40,000 feet and looks at the possibilities that lie ahead. He drops down to 20,000 feet to see what's in the way down the road. Going down to 5,000 feet lets him see each interpreter/translator and how they are succeeding. Based on what he has seen on the horizon, he figures out how to move people to and through the obstacles and opportunities. He communicates the vision and strategies in ways that evoke passion and commitment. Then, up he flies, to take followers into the unknown, coming back down when they lag, or stumble, become hesitant or lost. His "operating" altitude is at 20,000-40,000 feet.

Interpreter and translator leaders are often thought of as managers; their "operating" altitude is at 0-20,000 feet. She figures out how to implement processes and resources to achieve the vision and strategies. At 20,000 she can see everything within her area of responsibility. She spends hands-on time with first-level supervisors when she drops down to 3,000 feet. Making sure everyone knows where they're headed and that they understand why their activities connect and contribute to the vision and strategies. She also spends time on the ground making sure that followers are reassured by her presence. Always, she's adjusting and changing roles so that the right people, processes, and resources are in the right place at the right time. She is also giving feedback to the visionary leader about moving too quickly or too slowly.

Can one person be or do both? Absolutely!

Is one better or more necessary than the other? Absolutely NOT!

Both are essential for moving a company, education system, city, state, or nation forward. If you only have visionary leaders, you'll have great plans and strategies . . . and nothing will get done. If you only have interpreting leaders, you'll get lots of things done . . . and never go anywhere or accomplish anything new.

You spend time at higher altitudes because with height comes visibility. The chief officer in a battle fought to take command of the highest vantage point or was on horseback rather than on foot. Why? He could see further. See where the obstacles were located and how they were aligned to determine the best strategy for overcoming them. The commander (visionary) could relay the best counter-alignment and strategy for victory to his second-in-command (interpreter) who would break it down for the troops (followers).

In football, the defensive coordinator is usually stationed high in the arena, with a way to communicate to an assistant, who interprets and translates the vision and strategies to another coach or to the players.

The director of a theater production frequently sits high in the sound or light booth and relays vision and strategy to the choreographer who interprets and translates for the actors. Having a high vantage point allows her to see things she wouldn't see otherwise. The more clearly she can see what lies ahead, the better prepared her followers can be.

In this interplay between leading, managing, and supervising, each role is critical for achieving the vision, touchdown, or opening night hit.

So how do you know if you're visionary or interpretive, strategic or translating?

Does it matter? Do you have to be one or the other?

Why?

Who said so?

What makes you want to fit in a box anyway? Learn to be both, if you aren't already. Which, you probably are, you just might not be using all of your abilities. You might also be the visionary in one setting, and the translator in another.

One of my roles in Best Gurl inc, the multi-platform communication company I operate with my husband Thom, is interpreter/ translator. I figure out how to implement processes and resources to achieve Thom's vision and strategies. Another responsibility is making sure everyone associated with Best Gurl knows where we're headed and why their activities connect and contribute. I make sure everyone feels reassured and that the right people, processes, and resources are in the right place at the right time. I also give feedback to Thom about moving too fast or too slowly for our followers to keep up.

When I served on the Fort Walton Beach City Council, my primary role was visionary/strategist. We had a City Manager who was sometimes an interpreter/translator and at others a visionary/strategist. As Councilmembers, our primary role was to look at the possibilities that were ahead and figure out what was in the way of getting there. When we had a direction, it was up to us to communicate that vision in ways that evoked passion and commitment from the City employees, residents and business owners.

As the Executive Director for the National Association of Branch Campus Administrators (NABCA), I serve both roles with the voluntary Executive Committee and Members. Possibilities and direction. Implementation and resources.

I resent those who try to make others feel "less than" if they are interpreters/translators as though that's a "bad" thing. Without them, nothing would ever get done! For me, our organization, school, or family will never be "There Yet" until we grasp this fundamental and value all aspects of leadership.

So, how do you know if you're "There"? By flying high enough to be able to see where you've been, where you are, and where you're going . . . that gives vision. By flying close enough to know what to do about followers who are tired, discouraged, or lost . . . that's translation. By making sure that what you're giving is the highest quality. That's the only way those who follow you can be successful. Giving them less than you would demand for yourself, then expecting them to follow you day after day, year after year until you "Get There" is just silly! Eventually, they'll stop following altogether, or they'll pretend to be following while looking for a good exit ramp.

The adventure isn't at the destination; it's during the journey.

To "Get There" we need innovation and critical thinking, pioneers and settlers.

Where are you headed and is that the right direction for right now?

How do you get followers to go "There" when they don't want to go?

Asking the right questions is better than trying to make the smartest sounding statements . . . Asking the right questions is also essential for leadership . . . And leadership is for the fearless.

Everyone has to take responsibility and accountability for the vision and direction.

It's about bringing the right abilities to the job and delivering value every day.

Focus on what's doable, plan for what isn't yet.

Don't Fight
(. . . Win!!)

During a conversation I had with a newly hired CEO, he mentioned a conflict he'd been having with his counterpart at another organization. After describing the situation, he concluded with, "That's twice now, she's done that. One more time and we're through dealing with them." I thought about what he'd just said, then looked at him and replied, "There are no absolutes in leadership. You can't afford them. They are too costly in the long term." Then, I smiled.

Of course, there was silence, then, flashes of anger, thoughtfulness, and finally resolution flickered rapidly across his face. When I saw the presence of resolution, I continued. "They [the organization] are the only supplier of [the service] in this region. No one else does what you need. You can't afford to cut them off if you want to accomplish even half of what you envision. So, rather than draw a line in the sand that you can't defend, find a way to get what you need from them. As Sun Tzu wrote, 'Don't fight, win.'"

Our conversation continued and I proposed a sit down meeting with the CEO, the counterpart, and me. I was on his board of directors and had also hired him. Explaining further that, as the new CEO, he had no idea what kind of relationship existed before he was hired, and it wasn't fair to make a decision based on perception. He agreed.

You'll notice I rarely use words like "right" or "wrong" "good" or "bad." I find them narrow and judgmental. Most people try to force issues into colors . . . good is white (or yellow or green) bad is black (or red or orange). Life really isn't that simple.

For example, would it be "good or bad" for you to fight to protect the company you've built? Would it be "good or bad" for you to wage a really nasty political election campaign if your opponent acts like a jerk? Would it be "good or bad" for you to go after the murderer of your only child? Hmmm.

Very few things are *all* good or *all* bad. Most of us would agree that killing is "bad" right? But many people also favor the death penalty or going to war. "That's different," they'll tell me. Really? How? Killing is taking life away from another person by your own hand or decision. We create rationalizations or justifications, true . . . but for me, that makes the issue "gray."

My point is about a fundamental principle. There really are very few absolutes in relationships. It's never wise to draw emotional lines in the sand about anything. In this case, there was no legal or ethical issue so the only realistic option was to move the relationship to where it needed to be by remaining calm and deflecting anger. Usually, when someone is trying to get you to become angry, the calmer you get the angrier *they'll* get.

If you make every issue an Alamo, eventually just like the Alamo, you and your followers will fall. And then what?

Choose Your Battles
(. . . And Your Strategy)

Most of the time, being a leader means taking *The Road Less Traveled* [If you haven't read M. Scott Peck's book by the same title, add it to your reading list] and being faced with difficult choices or decisions. We encounter those situations, individuals, or obstacles that just won't go away; those challenges we face almost daily. In fact, you could spend all day every day doing nothing except dealing with challenges. Some are "fires" (petty). Most are "battles" (urgent). Every now and then, you run across one that is a "war" (mission critical).

There are challenges that are petty, "fires" that can easily be ignored. Bill and Sheri both want to use an empty file cabinet from the storage room. The outcome doesn't have any impact on the organizational vision. It's not worth your time to spend an hour or even 30-minutes mediating the dispute. Give the problem back to them and move on.

There are also urgent "battles" that are important but don't need to be solved right now. You're in the process of developing a presentation for your Board, Principal, or Stakeholders to roll out a new program or service. Henry, the Vice President of Finance comes to tell you that he has found a potential budget shortfall that will impact the organization next month unless changes are made before then. It's definitely worth solving, but you have three more weeks until next month. Although urgent, it's not mission critical yet. Plus, the new rollout is mission critical if you're going to continue to meet current demand and expand operations. Rather than interrupting what you're doing, have Henry put together some projections and possible solutions. Then, schedule a block of time after the presentation, but leaving enough time before the critical point, to meet with him. In other words, postpone.

Finally, there are mission critical "wars" that are very important, but they don't have to be solved by you. After you've dealt with Bill, Sheri and Henry, your Director of Personnel, Alice, comes in to tell you that a current employee has filed a discrimination lawsuit against the organization. The employee has not only filed suit, but he has already gone to print, broadcast and social media platforms. Alice is frantic.

This is definitely mission-critical and can negatively affect the outcome of every employee and corporate partner, not to mention the roll out. You can't ignore or postpone responding; however, you're not the legal or HR expert and you have an information officer for dealing with media. Knowing your limitations, you schedule a one-hour meeting with Alice (Human Resources), Joe (General Council) and Dana (Public Information). Share everything you know and have them share what they already know. Describe as specifically as possible how it impacts the organizational mission. Answer any questions they have, then give them until the end of the day to come back to you with a strategy. Make sure the entire organization knows to give them support and that the Board of Directors are aware. Then turn the task force loose to develop a war plan.

Every now and then, an attack on a strategic priority comes along. A war . . . It can come from ahead of or above you, from behind or below you, or from beside or inside you. When it does, you still have a choice. You can ignore it and keep on moving, slow down to dissect and analyze it, stop and collaborate with others to resolve it, or immediately strike to stop it.

Regardless how petty, urgent, or mission critical a challenge is, there are four questions you should think about addressing.

1. Is it worth solving? If not, then ignore it. If it is . . .

2. Does it have to be solved right now? If not, then schedule time to deal with it. If is does . . .

3. Do I know how to solve it? If you do, then choose your strategy and do what you need to implement it. If not . . .

4. Who is the best person to solve it? Stop what you're doing and get the right person or people together to focus on addressing the challenge.

Is it worth it, right now, do I know how, and am I the best? Taking a minute to think those through will save you countless hours, energy, and resources; keep you focused on the 40,000-foot vision and mission, and maintain your effectiveness.

If it can be fixed, replaced, done over, or done without . . . don't waste time and energy worrying about it. Instead, use your energy on vision, strategy, thinking, listening, and collaborating. Give up what you can't control. Focus on the cause, not the symptoms, because the truth is that the only thing we can control is how we respond to what happens around and to us. Otherwise, in the long run, you lose . . . and so do your followers.

Sometimes Silence
(. . . Is the Best Answer)

Become astute at reading the situation and determining the right approach so that you win for the greater, not the personal, good.

My husband is a former college football player. As a black student athlete, he helped integrate the Auburn University football team in 1970 and graduated in 1975 . . . it wasn't pleasant . . . he didn't go back.

In 2002, he received an invitation to the 30th year reunion of one of the University's greatest teams . . . he was working on a film in Los Angeles . . . I called to tell him about the invitation and read it to him.

"I'm not going," he said.

Now, I thought he needed to go. He was bitter and angry about the way he had been received and treated by the university, the athletic department, and by football in particular. He never really talked about what he experienced and I thought he needed to deal with it . . . all of it. There were a lot of things I could have said to him. I could have argued or disagreed; tried to talk him into going. Instead, I said *absolutely nothing*.

The silence lasted a long time . . .

"You think I should go," he said.

"I think you *need* to go . . . there's a difference," I told him.

38

We ended up going to the reunion and it was the best thing he could have done. It led to an ongoing relationship with his former teammates, the athletic department, and the university. In fact, from 2008 until 2016, he served on the University Foundation Board . . . the last two years as Chairman!

If I had argued, tried to convince, or nagged . . . he never would have gone. Sometimes, we have to let people come to their own conclusions instead of feeding it to them. When they do, it becomes their conclusion and conviction. One they will follow through and pursue to the end. Yet, we're so afraid of silence we forget that sometimes, it really is the best answer.

You Can't Win Them All
(. . . But You Don't Have to be a Sore Loser, Either)

Leadership means taking risks. Taking risks means you have a 50/50 chance of succeeding.

Let's face it; you won't always get it right the first time. Sometimes, especially if you're a risk taker, you'll make mistakes and face defeat when you're trying to achieve a vision. Those are the times when your true character will be most evident.

Martin Luther King Jr. once said, "The true measure of a [person's] character is not how [they] behave in times of comfort and convenience, but how [they] behave in times of discomfort and inconvenience." I agree!

I also think character includes how we deal with the aftershocks associated with disappointment and defeat.

When I was at the University of West Florida-Emerald Coast, we worked on a grant proposal that would bring thousands of dollars to our branch campus. Our vision was to provide the infrastructure for electronic student advising. The money would have allowed us to buy software licenses that let our academic and admissions advisors connect with our adult, working students via face-to-face technology using hardware and software that interfaced with admissions, registration, and student records. The savings in person-hours, missed phone calls, incorrect applications and forms, or other delays would have equaled hiring two more advisors . . . and saved our students so much in time and money.

After assembling and charging a small task force team, I monitored and assisted them for several weeks throughout the grant writing process. We had the final grant vetted by our internal research and development department then submitted the document on time, meeting the criteria. When the recipients of the grant were announced, we weren't on the award list. We were a runner up. The task force team was devastated. And I had several options.

I could have blamed the task force, R&D, or even the grant controller. I could have pointed to the times that the task force went in one direction and I advised another. Or, I could have held a meeting with the task force to discuss their feelings, allow them to vent and analyze our process and the winning responses. I also could have held a department meeting to announce the results. I could have brushed aside my own disappointment and defeat and launched myself and the team into the 'next project.' I could have allowed myself, and the task force team, to feel and progress through Denial, Anger, Blame, Depression/Sadness, and Acceptance. There were many responses I could have had. No matter how big or small the change people react the same . . . we grieve.

Some of those responses would have reflected my character; others would have reflected my grieving. Both would define me as a leader. What did I do? I chose to meet with the task force and together we grieved. We expressed our collective disbelief, were angry, blamed everyone and anyone, and talked about our sadness and disappointment. Then, we discussed what we would do next time. I also sent an email to the department to announce the results, praise the task force, share our disappointment, and define our strategy for going forward.

With disappointment and defeat, expect resistance and denial. Expect fear and depression. Expect blame and doubt. Expect reluctance and anger. Expect people to go through the stages of grieving when you introduce change or experience disappointment. Her first response is usually denial; "I can't believe they're moving the printers to one location. That makes no sense at all. I like my printer at my desk." The next response is usually anger; "I waste more time having to walk all the way over here to get what I've printed. Who came up with this stupid idea?" At some point, she gets to blame; "If Joe hadn't opened his big mouth and complained about how hard it is to service all the printers in our offices and what it cost for the ink, we wouldn't be in this mess. This is all his fault!" Depression creeps in, "Now that we've consolidated printers, what else will they consolidate? I bet my job is next. Then what will I do? I wish we could just go back to the way it was." Eventually, she gets to acceptance; "Why didn't we think of this before? The money we've saved on printing supplies and servicing was enough to upgrade all the computers in my department. This new laptop and monitor makes it so much easier when I travel. No more wondering which version is the newest, or trying to move things between two computers. This is great!"

You also need to recognize that sometimes the stages of grief pass quickly, a day or two, with small or minor changes. Bigger issues take longer for people to work their way to acceptance. It's really important not to initiate something new until everybody reaches acceptance on the current change. Otherwise, people get stuck at one or more stages without being able to work through their thoughts and feelings. Reality doesn't let you keep it nice and neat all the time, true; but, when you do get to decide, ask yourself if followers are ready for yet another round. Every good athletic coach knows when a player needs to come out of the game to recover.

Almost any magazine or book dealing with the subject of leadership must also deal with failure. They go together . . . you'll never learn to lead if you don't learn to fail.

So, how do you deal with failure? Again, by letting everyone feel what he or she feels, initially. That way, you're less likely to have long term regret, according to social psychologist and Professor of Marketing at Northwestern University, Neal Roese. While you want to allow yourself to feel, you don't want to stay there . . . don't wallow in, brood about, or be ashamed of the failure. In fact, the more mentors or others I tell, the faster I tend to figure out what I did wrong and what I can do about the responses I can control to choose a better direction.

When all else fails, do a search for "famous failures" and you'll be amazed at who pops up! People like Soichiro Honda, Socrates, Orville and Wilbur Wright, Abraham Lincoln, Lucille Ball, Sidney Poitier, Theodor Seuss Giesel, Igor Stravinsky, and Tom Landry. You'll realize that you're in very good company as long as you don't stop trying to achieve that goal, solve that problem, or build that contraption.

If You Always Do What You've Always Done
(. . . You'll Always Get the Same Results!)

Do you spend your days figuring out how to do things right, so you won't get in trouble or make mistakes? Or, do you spend your days figuring out the right things to do?

There is a difference.

When you're trying to always do something the 'right way' it's as though you're still in school taking a test. You're driven by fear of failure or embarrassment. You're also not making much progress. More likely you're going in a circle because no one is always right and most of the time there is someone who can do whatever it is better than you can. It gets frustrating when you can't figure it out. When you feel like you keep getting it wrong. When someone is always giving you feedback for improvement.

If you're nodding your head in agreement, or recognize the feedback giver in your life, take heart. You're not alone. I lived with it for more than 50 years.

My mom wasn't the kind of mother who always told me how wonderful and amazing I was. No matter what I did, she asked me two questions. First, Mommy asked, "Did you do your best?" If I said, "yes" she asked me, "Then, what would you change to do it even better next time?" If I said, "no" she asked me, "Then, what would you change to do your best next time?"

Aaaaaaggggggghhhhh!

At first, I thought that meant I was a failure, stupid, and that I wasn't doing whatever it was, well enough for her. In frustration one day, I asked her, "Why isn't anything I do ever good enough for you?" Then, I told her that since she would rather have another daughter, I'd just find somewhere else to live (yes, I was a teenager at the time!). With her usual calm and composure, The Princess Royal (aka my mother) looked at me, smiled, smoothed her hand down the side of my face, looked into my eyes and said, "You are the only daughter I have or want. Why wouldn't I want to help you become all that you can possibly be? Why wouldn't I give you every tool you could possibly need? Why would I send you out into the world unprepared for the choices and decisions you have to make? This isn't about you getting the right answer joyce; this is about you learning to choose the right things to do."

Over time, my answers to Mommy's first question began to change. When she asked, "Did you do your best?" I began to respond differently. "Yes, because the other options wouldn't have let me reach my goal (or it would have affected someone else)." Sometimes I would say, "No, because if I hadn't wasted time getting ready this morning, I wouldn't have had to rush and wouldn't have missed the bus, been late to school, and missed the test." She was teaching me to choose between doing things right (for approval) and doing the right things (for results). Make sure you give that to your followers. Everybody needs a "feedback giver" to keep us from doing the same things over and over again.

It's really hard to give feedback about a mistake or failure to perform. So, here's a handy process I call "The DESC Broken Record." DESC stands for "Describe," "Express," "State," and "Convey." First, you describe the behavior, rather than talk about the person. Then, express how the behavior makes you and others feel. State exactly what you want or don't want to happen in the future. Last, convey the consequences of performing and not performing as desired. This one is really important. Don't make threats and don't convey consequences you either won't or can't carry out. The Broken Record is just what it sounds like . . . it plays the same tune over and over again.

I'll use a real example to show you what I mean . . .

Back in the ancient days before cell phones, I had a young follower named "Frank." He was brilliant at his job and had a charming personality. He had the foundation to be a great employee and someday a wonderful leader. And he was almost always late to work!

After keeping track of exactly what time he was at his desk, ready to begin working every day for 10 days, I called Frank into my office. "Frank, for the last two weeks, you have not been at your desk ready to work at 7:30 am, eight times. That frustrates me, makes me angry, and isn't fair to your co-workers who are ready to work at 7:30 am. I need you to be *at* your desk, *ready* to work at 7:30 am *every* morning . . . not entering the parking lot . . . not getting your coffee . . . not chatting with your buddies in another department . . . at your desk, ready to work. If you do that, then you and I don't ever have to have this conversation again. If you don't, then our next conversation won't be as pleasant as this one." Then, I remained silent.

Of course, Frank began explaining and rationalizing about how it was only once in a while, that he really wasn't late if he was on the premises, that he had a new baby who kept him up at night . . . I waited until he was finished, then I said, "Frank, for the last two weeks, you have not been at your desk ready to work at 7:30 am, eight times. That frustrates me, makes me angry, and isn't fair to your co-workers who *are* ready to work at 7:30 am. I need you to be *at* your desk, *ready* to work at 7:30 am *every* morning . . . not entering the parking lot . . . not getting your coffee . . . not chatting with your buddies in another department . . . at your desk, ready to work. If you do that, then you and I don't ever have to have this conversation again. If you don't, then our next conversation won't be as pleasant as this one." Then, I remained silent . . . again.

This happened at least two more times before Frank finally figured out that I wasn't budging or arguing with him. "Okay, I'll be on time at my desk, ready to work at 7:30 am," he said. And he was, for about three weeks. Then, I received a phone call one morning at about 7:20 from someone in another department. "Hey joyce, Frank flagged me down on the highway to make me promise to tell you that he is changing a flat tire and will be here as soon as he finishes," the male voice told me. At about 7:32 am, Frank rushed in! Yes, we had a conversation and yes, I documented the incident in his personnel file . . . because I told him the consequence and needed to demonstrate that I meant it. I think it was more than a year later that Frank wasn't at his desk, ready to work at 7:30 am again! Today, Frank is an excellent leader and has a successful professional career.

"Why Are They Following *Me*?"

CHARACTER & REPUTATION

Character describes your mental and moral qualities. Reputation is what others believe to be true about you.

My best lessons are learned through watching and processing in my mind. Always more observer than talker, I watched others as a child and young adolescent. I saw what was effective and what wasn't. Watching others taught me that when you wanted people to do something, you had to answer "Why?" It taught me that you couldn't *make* people do what you asked; you had to make them *want* to do what you asked them to do. Watching others taught me that pride and arrogance brought resentment and envy, not admiration.

I learned that not speaking up doesn't result in you being lifted up by others; it only results in being stepped on. Lay on the floor like a rug and no one *ever* picks you up and hangs you on a wall . . . they do what we do with rugs . . . wipe their feet (or walk all over you)! Watching taught me about being assertive—not aggressive or passive. Answering "Why?" before telling "How." I learned to choose which ones, when, and who goes, in terms of battles or challenges. To let others know how much you care instead of how much you know. How to step up and do the dirty work as well as the easy or glamorous tasks. These observations, and the results they produced, became the foundation for my future. They became (and are *still* becoming) my character.

Being the owner, supervisor, CEO, or parent doesn't only mean you get to tell people what to do. It means you're responsible for making sure everyone who follows you has what they need and knows how to be successful. It also means cleaning up your messes and keeping track of who needs a little more attention. Making sure they have what they need to be successful and operate at the highest level. Learning who you are and becoming who you were meant to be. Fulfilling your purpose by leading others into their own discovery.

Who am I at my worst? That's a really important question. Who we are at our worst is usually the person those who are closest to us know. Why is it that we tend to give our best behavior and consideration to those we may never see again, at the same time we do and say things in front of those closest to us that we would never want others to hear or see? The way I behave when I think no one important is watching is who I really am.

Ouch!!

When are you most proud of yourself? Is it when you've done something wonderful and everyone knows about it? Is it when you're receiving public recognition? Or is it when you connect two people who would never have met and the result is an extraordinary achievement or breakthrough . . . and no one but the three of you know that you were involved? Are you most proud of yourself when you work to make the right things happen and never seek credit?

There is no wrong or right answer.

Before I speak or act, ask, "Is it truthful, necessary, and kind?" The Rotary 4-way Test asks the questions: Is it true? Is it fair to all concerned? Will it build good will and better relationships? Will it be beneficial to all concerned?

"I don't know," are three of the most important words you can say. The other three are, "I was wrong."

Allow yourself to be vulnerable.

Let go of "doing" and focus on "being" and "becoming."

"The only way to win is to focus not on what you achieve, but who you become as a consequence of the chase," wrote Jim Loehr, performance psychologist and Co-Founder of the Johnson & Johnson Human Performance Institute. I agree.

Earning followers isn't a one-shot proposition. You have to constantly earn the respect and commitment of followers. People always have the choice to not follow. They can stop, and stay exactly where they are, or turn around and go back where they came from. If you are wise you'll never forget that.

What kind of leader are you and who is following you? The answers define your character and your reputation.

Leadership Can be Lonely
(. . . So, You'd Better Like Yourself!)

After being elected to the City Council of Fort Walton Beach, a small rural city, I discovered an interesting phenomenon about people and followers. When there was a large, controversial issue on the agenda, the Council Chamber was packed. But, on a meeting-by-meeting basis, not a soul could be found except the staff members who had to be there. The strange thing was, people would tell me about things we discussed, or decisions we made when I was in the grocery store or running errands around town. How? They watched on TV at home!

Leadership is lonely.

Flying at 40,000 feet is a solitary effort. Yes, it's quiet. Yes, you can see farther ahead. Yes, there are no distractions. But, you can't hear the voices of encouragement, either. You can't see the faces of determination and trust. There aren't others to fly along and help buffer the force of the wind.

Eagles fly alone and ducks fly in formation. There's a reason for that.

An eagle's wingspan allows for soaring heights and greater lift. A duck's wings are short. Eagles fly through and above the storm clouds. Ducks take cover.

"Cows run away from a storm. Buffalos run toward a storm. The buffalo gets through the storm first," former Cherokee Nation Chief Wilma Mankiller said. I've pretty much always been a buffalo. I got into more trouble by heading into storms! Tell me I can't and watch me. Tell me it's impossible and I'll figure out how or who can. Tell me it's useless to try and I'll become *Don Quixote* (laughing).

How do you know whether you are a leader or a follower? An eagle or a duck? A cow or a buffalo? Who picks the person we ultimately call leader?

If you think you are a leader, but really aren't sure, take this little test. Look behind you.

If no one is following, you're a one-person band.

If the only ones following are direct reports who are there because they have to be, you're a supervisor with a title.

If the only ones following are sycophants who tell you only what you want to hear, you're a bully.

Leaders are people others want to follow, *volunteer* to follow, and *take risks* to follow.

I believe we're all leaders on some level or in some situation. The difference is who we lead and how.

For example, let's say that one parent assumes the role for primary childcare in the home and the other plays a major role outside the home. The one at home with the child is the child's leader. The other is leading outside the home. Same skills and same characteristics; they both need vision and strategy to reach the destination. Both need to love, solve problems, resolve conflicts, and make decisions. The only difference is who they lead and how. Neither has "the more important" role.

One of the most difficult lessons to learn is that not everybody will follow you. Some people believe that with the right vision – the

right direction – the right information and skill – and the right re-
sources – then everyone will follow. Not!!

Let me ramble for a minute . . .

Behaviorists will tell you that there are three reasons people
don't do what you want or expect them to do: They don't know
how. They don't have the right tools, equipment, or environment.
They don't want to.

If you've explained to followers where you want them to go and
why they're going, how they'll be supported and cared for on the
journey and they have everything they need for the trip and they
still don't go with you; then they just don't want to follow. There is
absolutely nothing you can do about that. It may be that they don't
want to follow *you* and it wouldn't matter where you were going. It
could be they don't want to *go* where you're going and it wouldn't
matter who you are. Either way, they aren't coming and they're hold-
ing everybody else back.

Henry David Thoreau wrote, "The one who stands alone can
leave today; but the one who travels with another must wait until
they are ready to go." So, if you're going to be effective, you have
to know when it's time to walk away from a follower. Don't waste
energy, effort, and resources trying to make someone do what he or
she has already decided they don't want to do. It's not worth it to
you and it's really not fair to everybody else. Making that decision is
sometimes hard and always lonely.

The Upward Moving Spiral
(. . . Learning to Lead With Wisdom)

Although this isn't a religious book, I've learned from the study of various philosophies and religions that there are a few consistent and universal truths. Indeed, some of you who read this would think that many of these truths include characteristics that everyone should possess. As far as I'm concerned, you would be right.

J. I. Packer, author of *Knowing God*, wrote, "Wisdom is the power to see and the inclination to choose, the best and highest goal, together with the surest means of attaining it. Wisdom is, in fact, the practical side of moral goodness." I agree.

Because we naturally and instinctively want our own way, before we can really be used to lead, we must be taught to follow. I don't know about you, but for me that learning process usually comes as the result of three steps: doing it my way, falling flat on my face, and realizing I can't do it myself (laughing . . . again).

Two points.

First, this whole "becoming a leader" adventure is not a one-time, once-and-for-all activity. It's like an upward revolving spiral, always moving, and always turning.

Second, the reality is that until we are humble enough to know how incapable of leading we are, we'll never be successful.

So, how does the spiral work? Usually, I encounter a situation, individual, or challenge that those who have chosen to follow me must respond to or overcome. So, I take up my "Awesome gossom

Battle-Ax" and charge in swinging (yes, I really do have one . . . Jo-
anna made it for me!). Usually, I'm righteously angry because "How
dare it/they get in the way of My followers? Who do they think they
are? Don't they know I will go down swinging on behalf of My fol-
lowers? Did they really think they'd get away with it and *I* wouldn't
do anything?"

. . . Well, you get the picture. Usually, at this point, Joanna (or
Geoffrey before her) would sit me down and talk me down . . . some-
times they were successful! Other times . . . not so much.

But remember, we're all capable of operating with wisdom and in
order to keep us moving upward towards that fulfillment, we must
be prepared and tried, tested and humbled. That means when I (and
those who have chosen to follow me) encounter the situation, indi-
vidual, or challenge I can't always just snatch-up my battle-ax and
go fight! It's usually there for a reason. Most of the time, there is
something I need to learn, relearn, remember, or apply. Until I do
that, the only place I'm going is flat on my face. So, every now and
then I recognize and remember not to just charge into the situation.
At those times, in those moments, I reflect on what the circumstance
is designed to teach me instead of focusing on the circumstance it-
self. Remembering that circumstances and situations are designed to
help me develop wisdom lets me bypass the need to do it my way and
fall on my face. It reminds me I can't do this on my own because the
lesson isn't mine to teach, it's mine to learn. And there is the key to
the whole wise leadership thing . . . I'm not always the teacher; I'm
also the learner.

That means . . .

Instead of wasting all that energy and time, I can immediately
ask what scrubbing up or what service do I need to provide in this

circumstance? Then, I can wait for the guidance and direction that, for me, only comes in a still small voice when I'm quiet and waiting. Then, I know whether or not this is a circumstance worth dealing with; if this is the time to deal with it; and if I am the right one to deal with it or if someone else needs to take over. Leading with wisdom is seeing, choosing, and attaining the best and highest for everyone involved.

I *wish* I could tell you that one day you will be able to lead completely with wisdom every time and every day. Ha! I wish *I* could do it, let alone tell *you* how. But, I can't. It's that pushy spiral of life that just gets in the way. Every time I think I'm "wise" and get cocky or just comfortable, that darn spiral keeps revolving and I end up at the same lesson (Grrrr). . . only harder or trickier to identify. Does that make sense?

For me, the circumstance and people are usually different. Most of the time the consequences are different as well. But somehow, guess who keeps running into the same old character traits? Patience, unselfish love, humility (get that one a lot), kindness (another of my frequent visitors), goodness, self-control, joy (that one isn't often, but when it comes, it packs a punch), peace, faithfulness, and gentleness all add up to wisdom. You might think that I'd "get it" faster as the spiral revolves and the lessons recur. Nope! That's not the point. The point is in the recognition. Realizing and being reminded once again that I can't "fix" this circumstance or person, never could, and never will. Whatever "this" is, I'm supposed to learn from it.

Developing character is not for the faint of heart or timid. In fact, developing character period is daunting. Why? Because the only way to develop character is to willingly allow yourself to be placed in situations that demand the use of the very character you're trying to develop!.

Huh?!

Let me explain another way.

One year I decided that I was going to focus on developing wisdom through the character traits associated with the Fruit of the Spirit. You know, those nine characteristics the Apostle Paul described in the Bible book of Galatians: love, joy, peace, patience, kindness, goodness, faithfulness, gentleness, and self-control. I figured if I worked on one each month, I'd have them mastered by the end of the year.

Hah!

The first month my focus was on "love." Every morning I read and meditated on a passage from inspirational and spiritual books, trying to learn what love really meant and looked like in action. Each day that month, my purpose was to love those who crossed my path and to express love in everything I did. January began and the month continued something like this . . .

4 January – Had a *huge* blow-up with family members.

20 January – Planned to have a "me" day and ended up cleaning our house to put it on the market.

30 January – Had an argument with my husband over something stupid (that we can't even remember).

By the end of January, I who prided myself on being a loving person, wife, mother, daughter, friend, and sister, was sick of *every single person* in my life and was ready to throw *everyone* off a bridge!

Realizing that I hadn't mastered love at all, let alone understood it, I decided to "give it another month." After all, there were only 9 fruits and 12 months, right?!?

Unfortunately, or fortunately as it turned out, February was no better. We won't even talk about the Valentine's Day I had that year. Ugh!

I realized, near the end of February that I was less loving than I had been in December! What the heck was going on?

As February turned into March, then April, and I was *still* stuck on "love," it finally dawned on me that I was being given opportunities to love when it wasn't my natural response; that my character was being forged, like metal in a fire. I also began to see that I would never "master" love. Instead, on the last day of that year, I realized that what I had developed was the ability to recognize when love was and wasn't evident in my words, thoughts, and actions. That's character development!

Eleven years later, [Yes, I know there are only nine fruit. I had to spend more than one year on a few . . . No, I won't tell you which ones!!] I had finally struggled through "self-control." I was exhausted.

I had been heated and forged, trying to learn to be instead of *do*. I could recognize when I wasn't *being* in the moment. Even if sometimes I chose to ignore myself!

So, use my cautionary tale as an example when you begin to examine yourself for the presence or absence of wisdom. Take it from me, when you do – life is guaranteed to get hot!

What in the world does any of this have to do with leadership? Easy. We're all leading someone; a child, spouse, friend, neighbor, someone. It doesn't require a congregation, university, corporation, or country. As long as some *one* is willingly following you, you're leading. As long as you've been entrusted with the responsibility, you're going to be refined. That's just the way it is. Don't ask me why; I didn't make the universe (laughing)!

Whether you believe in a deity like Jehovah, Yahweh, Allah, God, or Trinity; whether you believe in a higher power like Wind, Nature, Earth, or Fire; whether you don't believe in anything other than what you can see and touch. There is something within every single person that asks and needs to be loved, to be special, to be important. We seek to fulfill that need in many ways, some effectively in the short term, some not effectively at all. But we keep trying.

Usually doing the same things that already haven't worked.

. . . If you always do what you've always done . . . !?!

Somehow, until we realize that we cannot fulfill the need for love, being special, and being important on our own, we'll spend our lives running on a wheel like a gerbil in a cage. Never getting anywhere. That's really the first step. Acknowledging that you're not in control and that you can't even fulfill your most basic and fundamental needs. Once you can wrap your brain around that concept, thought, and feeling you're ready to be taught how to lead with wisdom.

Until you get to that point, I'd just put this book down and go find something else to read if I were you. Otherwise, you're just going to get frustrated.

If you have the glimmers of thinking, "You know she may have a point. Everything I've done so far hasn't resulted in me leading in a way that makes my followers (or me) feel loved, special, or important. Maybe I'm doing this backwards . . . " Then keep reading!

Fearless Leadership
(. . . Takes the Road Less Traveled)

A leader often finds herself on *The Road Less Traveled* (M. Scott Peck again!). There are no road signs, mile markers, or speed limits. There is nothing except her and the road, headed in a direction where she's not sure where she is going, but she knows that where she is going has something better to offer than where she came from.

Sometimes, she is able to convince others to follow her on this road. Follow when she isn't sure where they're going, can't answer how long they'll be on the road, and isn't sure what she'll find when they get there. Convincing others to journey with her, to take a chance, and to take a risk because the destination, and the journey, offers something better. Being willing to demand excellence from herself and her followers. That's fearlessness.

The CEO of JP Morgan asks the question, "Would you want your child working for you?"

WOW!!

When I read that, I thought about a 3rd grade teacher in one of my mother's schools. Mommy said "Mrs. J" was a horrible teacher and that the children's scores, behavior, and attitude were a reflection of her inability. Yet, no one had ever written a disciplinary evaluation or letter about her.

It took an entire year of classroom visits and observations. A year of feedback sessions and action planning. Mom spent an entire year documenting every single thing, and then she filed the paperwork to have Mrs. J removed from her school. Everyone was shocked;

teachers, assistant principals, staff, even the folks at central office . . .
There was no way this was going to happen in the Chicago Public
School System! Mrs. J had tenure, was a long-time member of the
teacher's union and her husband was a very powerful executive with
a national company. She was "untouchable," everyone told Mom.

Mommy just smiled.

I could have warned Mrs. J to watch out . . . That smile is deadly!

At the hearing, Mrs. J's union attorney questioned her about her
degrees and years of experience. He asked about her evaluations and
performance ratings, leading her to the statement that the principal
didn't like her and was unfairly singling her out. It was a brilliant ar-
gument supported by the glowing evaluations from former principals
and lack of complaints from parents.

Then it was Mom's turn. She stood at the table and looked at the
teacher. "Good morning, Mrs. J," Mom said to her. "Good morning,"
the teacher replied curtly. Mom smiled, "I just have one question, if
I may. I know that you have two grandchildren who are in elemen-
tary school." Mom paused as Mrs. J looked confused. "Would you be
satisfied if your grandchildren received the same quality of education
as your 3rd graders?" Mom finished, still smiling. Without missing a
beat, Mrs. J drew herself up, looked at Mommy as if she'd grown a
second head and replied, "*Of course not!*"

Mommy looked at the disciplinary panel, nodded her head,
smiled, said, "Thank you. I have no further questions," and sat back
down.

It took a few minutes for the teacher (and the union attorney) to
figure out what just happened. By the time they did, the panel had

finished deliberating and rendered their decision. Not only was Mrs. J removed from Mom's school, she was fired from the system and her City-specific license was permanently revoked!

If you wouldn't want your children, grandchildren, niece or nephew to have the same quality of service, resources, or product you're providing . . . If you want your followers to be innovative and risk taking, quality producing and focused on the future . . . Blaze your own trail! Fix what is broken! Be fearless and courageous!

Learning to be courageous can be a daunting undertaking, so get some inspiration from Sandra Ford Walton's book, *Courage*. You won't be sorry!

The Harder My Head
(. . . The More It Hurts!)

Being determined and fearless can be strengths . . . or weaknesses. As a leader, you'd better figure out when they are and when they aren't so you can respond correctly. Usually, going right along with determination and fearlessness is the belief that we can do everything on our own, without any help from others. That gets us in trouble as well!

When I believe in something, or know that someone is depending on me, I'm stubborn and fearless.

Ask anybody who really knows me.

If I believe strongly in or about something, you can't make me do or not do the opposite. My mom said she discovered that when I was two years old.

We lived in Hyde Park, Chicago and went to the beach or museum every day, had a picnic lunch, then did grocery shopping and came home. Because this was Hyde Park, we walked . . . well, Mom walked; I rode in my stroller when I was two (laughing!). On this particular day, we got back home and Mommy had the stroller, beach bag, our grocery bag, and me. So, she stood me in front of the steps and told me to go up. I refused. Told her I was too tired. She used that "Mommy" voice and told me again. I refused . . . again.

Finally, Mommy patted my bottom to "push" me all the way up the steps, one step at a time, carrying everything on one arm! She always burst out laughing when she got to this part, "By the time we got up the stairs and to our door, my arms were aching, I was

66

exhausted, and you were even angrier. You got to the door, turned around, looked at me and said, 'I'm sick and tired of you!'" Usually, at this point, Mommy was laughing so hard she couldn't speak. "I looked at you in astonishment and said, 'joyce, what did you say?' knowing that I had to be mistaken," she would continue. "'I said, I'm sick and tired of you!'" Whomever she was telling the story to would gasp and usually look at me as if surprised that I was still alive, especially if they knew her well (giggle).

Mommy would finish, "I couldn't believe that a two year old could leave me speechless, so I just told you to go to your room!" [I got sent to my room . . . a lot!] That day, I also got spanked on my little bottom, so I didn't say that again . . . out loud, at least!

Fearless . . . Determined . . . and in so much Trouble!

Cheryl Jones is a very dear friend and one of the most talented musicians and songwriters I've ever heard. She is also one of the most giving. Cheryl called me one day to ask if she could borrow my ear for a few minutes. She began telling me about all of the project balls she was currently trying to keep in the air. Cheryl was working on the music and lyrics for new album material, she was teaching five classes a semester at a local college. She had twenty students in private voice or instrumental lessons (she plays several instruments). Her husband wanted to go out of town for "us time," she was director of the very popular and in-demand college Jazz Band, and she was finishing up her doctoral dissertation. On top of all that, Cheryl was having physical problems that began small but that, by now, developed into something more serious and her doctor wanted her to see a specialist.

Her giving nature had almost become a liability. Cheryl giggled in her wonderful way that always makes me smile. We shared a laugh, and chatted about saying no when we need to and not taking on more than we should. We have had this talk with each other several times during our years of friendship. Sometimes I was the recipient. Today was her turn.

"Right now, my health is what I need to focus on. Everything else can wait or be done by someone else," she said. I smiled and told her to let me know what the specialist said.

Years later when we talked about that conversation, I reminded Cheryl about my run-in with the doctor who wanted me in the hospital because I had contracted pneumonia. I kept arguing with him about the workshops and clients who were depending on me and about the things I needed to do with my son that week. I just didn't have time to be in the hospital! I had people depending on me and I was the only one who could do everything. Finally, the doctor looked at me and said, "joyce, you have a fever of 105°, fluid in both lungs, and you are almost completely dehydrated. If you lay down and go to sleep tonight, you won't wake up!"

I went to the hospital . . . and never let myself get to that point again.

Stubborn and fearless, giving and determined . . . Yes. Stupid? No!!

Push Your Chair In
(. . . And Clean Up Your Own Mess!)

My Grandpa Golden used to say, "¿Si puedes hacer algo lindo, por qué no?" (Loose translation: If you can do something kind or nice for someone and it doesn't take anything away from you, what's the harm?). Mostly, he would just look at me and say, "¿Nieta, Por qué no?" when I was grumbling about something Mommy wanted me to do for somebody else.

Huh?!

How you treat people, especially the ones you don't see as "important" and how you behave toward them says so much about who you really are. Remember socks before shoes?!?

Making unnecessary work for others means they have less time to focus on things that are urgent (moving a project along) rather than petty (cleaning up your mess) and almost no time to work on what is mission critical and strategic (lining up goals and plans to reach that new market) rather than petty (pushing your chair back in).

My mom used to tell me that the two most powerful positions in any organization are administrative and custodial. I thought she was crazy . . . until I went for a meeting with a potential CEO client. I watched his assistant keep people on hold before she connected them and she ignored everyone who came into the waiting area for at least 90 seconds. There were cobwebs in corners and dust on top of picture frames. So what? Pretty much everyone who finally saw or talked with him was already irritable. And, since his behavior was arrogant and obnoxious, it didn't make for good or productive conversations. What's more, he had no clue why there were project delays or high turnover, which was why he was considering a consultant in the first place!

Nope.

Didn't take the client.

Won't work with or for people whose behavior I don't like.

. . . But I did tell him how to fix his problem (smile).

Turns out, Mom was right! Try to host a customer, student, or board member when the trash hasn't been emptied for days, or the carpet vacuumed or the room dusted. Imagine how long you would be able to function if your phone messages never got to you, your email gets deleted, or you aren't told that someone was waiting for you. Do you know the name of the building custodian or the name of any clerical person other than your own? When was the last time you simply said, "Thank you" to either of them? Or left a note and a snack for the custodial staff?

I'm usually curious in a room of leaders. I like to see how they behave because it tells me so much more about their style than their words, ideas, or accomplishments ever could. I like to see who picks up their accumulated litter of coffee cup, napkin, or crumbs before leaving a conference table. I like to see who sits at the head of the conference table and who sits in the middle or along the wall. My favorite is seeing who pushes in their chair when the meeting is over and they are standing to leave the room. I think that action alone tells me almost everything I need to know about someone, as a person, as a communicator, and especially as a leader.

Okay, you're scratching your head, wondering what in the world pushing your chair in has to do with leadership. It's simple, really. Good leaders are aware of their followers. Great leaders never create extra unproductive work for their followers and they lead by example. They know that a huge part of their responsibility is clearing the path and lighting the trail so that followers know and can see where they're going and can get there without being sidetracked or slowed down.

Great leaders know that when they leave their litter on the table after a meeting, someone (hint, hint, a follower) must take time to clean it up. Great leaders know that when they leave their chair out at the conference table, someone (hint, hint, a follower again) has to push it back in. That detracts from the follower's primary responsibility for achieving the vision.

"Wait a minute," I can almost hear you saying. "It doesn't take but a minute to clear away cups and napkins or push in a chair." Exactly!! So why can't the person who made the mess or sat in the chair put it to rights when he is finished? "¿Por qué no?" Arrogant leadership! A true oxymoron. He assumes that it's, "someone else's job" to take care of that minor detail. Yet he would be infuriated to enter his conference room to find it exactly as he left it.

Why?

Let's say the follower is a member of the maintenance or custodial staff. Her vision is to maintain the most efficient and beautiful physical environment possible for workers and guests. Now, would you rather have her spending the shift making sure coffee cups are tossed and chairs are pushed in, or would you rather have her polishing the table to a high gloss shine and wiping cobwebs out of the corners? Would you rather have her wiping crumbs or dusting picture frames? Tossing napkins or polishing elevator panels? Picking up papers beside trashcans or identifying ways to streamline building or office upkeep, cutting and placing fresh flowers in beautiful vases throughout the building, or even washing windows and windowsills?

The point is that the things that take an organization from average to good and *From Good To Great* requires several things, as author Jim Collins describes. None of which can be or are done when followers feel taken for granted or treated as less than. None of which are done when followers are compliant rather than committed. It requires commitment to the organizational vision and feeling part of that vision. It requires knowing and seeing everyone doing their part to achieve that vision. It requires believing his contributions make a difference and help make it easier for his co-followers to move closer to achieving that vision. It requires trust, commitment, and equity. Without those in place, all you have is compliance. Followers will show up, usually right on time and no earlier, they will do the job they're specifically told to do, and they will ignore or overlook anything that is perceived as "extra."

That's why great leaders push in their chair.

What do you want your headstone to say? "She treated everyone with courtesy and respect," or "He never put the seat down." Then live that way now!

Close the door.

Turn off the lights.

Wipe it up.

Use a tissue (or handkerchief) to blow your nose.

Clean your room.

Don't take more than you can eat.

Say "Please" and "Thank you."

Treat everyone like royalty.

Pick it up and put it away.

Mind your E's and E's (Etiquette and Elegance).

Etiquette is making others feel comfortable around you, not showing them that you know some arbitrary list of rules.

Elegance is being true to who you are while bringing out the best in others. Medical philanthropist and fashion icon, Deeda Blair is a great example of this. Most people would dismiss her if she walked into their office. There is nothing about her that screams, "Pay attention to me, I'm brilliant and important," (which she is . . .). Instead, she focuses on others . . . bringing out the best they have to offer.

Susan Amat, founder and CEO of Venture Hive (an accelerator for economic development) runs her entire company by what she calls the "No Jerk Rule"!

Is Anybody Following
(. . . Because They Want To?)

Growing up I sometimes saw examples of, "Being the leader means being in charge. Having other people do what they're told." But in my very first job, I learned that regardless of the threat, people only do what they want to do!

My first real job (other than babysitting) was in a neighborhood dry cleaner and laundry. I was hired to be a cleaner and presser at age 16 for $1.25 an hour! I also waited on customers who came in to drop off or pick up their laundry and cleaning, carefully counting out the change from the old-fashioned cash register and writing out the receipt. I was so excited. Looking back, I must have been a nut . . . it was summer time in a building filled with washers and dryers, pressers and boilers . . . and no air conditioning! Anyway, I would get to work early every day, usually riding my bike or walking the mile from home.

After I'd worked for about a month, "Joe," the owner, came in during my slow Sunday afternoon shift to tell me that his family was going out of town for a two-week vacation and that I would be responsible while they were gone. Why me?! There were others who'd been there longer than me and I was one of the youngest employees.

Joe gave me the keys, bank bag and deposit slips, and the employee schedule, including everyone's hourly rates. I was to pay myself $1.50 an hour while I was "in charge." Believe it or not, even at that age, the money didn't help me feel better about the whole thing. First step for me . . . talk to Mommy and get advice!

After a staff meeting the next day, to let everyone know what was going on, Joe was gone.

During the next two days I talked with each of the four other employees about what they needed to do their job, what I needed from them, and why they were important. Everyone had settled in and worked really hard by the end of the first week. When I got to work that Saturday morning, I paid myself, then walked down to the bakery and bought a dozen doughnuts. I put them on a pretty plate I'd brought from home and wrote a little sign that said, "Thank you for working so hard this week." (Thanks Mommy!)

I'll never forget that day. As people came in and found the plate, I could hear them talking. At the end of the day, all the doughnuts were gone – I hadn't gotten any! But, that day, and the rest of the following week, no one was late, no one left early, no one took longer than they were supposed to for lunch, and everyone worked harder than I'd ever seen them work. I bought a little cake and some juice for the last Saturday before Joe and his family returned. This time, there was a tiny sliver of cake left for me at the end of the day; but, everyone hugged me and thanked me as they left for the night.

When Joe came in on Sunday afternoon, I turned over the keys, payroll tickets, deposits, and other information I had for him. He asked how things had gone and I told him they'd been fine. I never told him that I'd bought doughnuts or cake and he never asked me about it. On Monday after I finished my shift and was waiting to be relieved, I realized that the person who was supposed to replace me was late. She hadn't been late for two weeks! When she finally got to the cleaners, she looked sheepish as she apologized. "Why are you late? You haven't been late in two weeks!" I said. "Because," she said with a grin, "you cared and he doesn't. You were here early and worked until everything was done, he just comes in to clean out the cash register, yell at us for mistakes, and tell us what to do."

It was another lesson that has stayed with me. It's not about what you gain with leadership, but what you're willing to give up. He takes the last slice of pie, or none, so that his followers are full and well nourished.

She makes sure her followers aren't struggling to get to the campus, assembly line, or teller window from a far away, muddy or unpaved parking lot, especially when she has a designated spot right by the door!

He looks for dangers so followers can move constantly forward.

I know this isn't always the modern belief and practice. That's okay. Radical ideas have changed the world (smile). I still believe you will never be as effective until you learn to be last, sacrifice for followers, and let them get the praise.

You don't declare yourself to be a leader, and then try to convince people to follow you. It doesn't take talking the loudest – or the most – or knowing all the answers. You discover that you're a leader when you realize there are people depending on you, looking at you for direction, trusting you to get them there safely. Leaders are courteous, generous, and selfless. Those pretending to be are egotistical, prideful, and need to be the center of attention.

Give the people you want as followers the answers to . . . Why? Where? How? and What? . . . Give them vision, direction, information and skill, and resources . . .

I think, most important and critical is giving the answer to "Why?"

That answer is . . . *Vision*.

Until people understand why you want them to do something new or go in a different direction, you can't go anywhere. If followers don't trust the truth of the "why," believe in the "where," and have the "how" and "what," leadership doesn't survive.

Why are they following you? Is it because of your title or position in their lives? Is it because they believe in your vision for the future or your destination? Is it because it's easier or faster for them to hitch themselves to your wagon and let you do the pulling? Is it because they just want to go wherever you go? Is it because you talked them into following you with the promise of what they would receive at the end of the journey?

Some people follow grudgingly . . . because of where you're going; . . . because you've convinced them; or . . . they have no choice because you have more power than they do. That can be a dangerous thing. Remember, author J. I. Packer described how critical it is for power to be ruled by wisdom. I agree. Power without wisdom can be dangerous.

Absolute power with impunity has led to the most unspeakable evils in the world. It is terrifying. Think of all the situations where someone, or a group of some ones, had absolute power with impunity . . . Nazis in Germany, Slave owners in the US, Hutus in Rwanda, Roman-Catholic Priests with Children, Mao Zedong and the Chinese, the Christian and Muslim Crusades, Nestle and Wal-Mart labor practices, the ExxonMobil and British Petroleum oil spills . . . you get the picture. This kind of power gives good and generous people a platform for doing what they would ordinarily never do.

As far as I'm concerned, the only real reason for people to follow you out of commitment is that they believe in you; otherwise, you're just an emperor with no clothes. Why are they following me? That's the $64,000,000 question. I work on my answer every day . . . and share some of them with you here. What's your answer?

Leadership Generosity
(. . . And Authority)

In a discussion of the why's and how's of leadership, there is one attribute many shy away from. That is the character and nature of being a righteous and moral judge.

We want to think of ourselves as benevolent, tolerant, loving, and kind. All of which should be true. Yet, in a discussion about knowing how to effectively lead, we also have to recognize and pay attention to judgment. Goodness. Fairness. Authority. Wisdom. Power.

In a final tribute to author J. I. Packer, he discusses four attributes that I believe apply to leadership.

First, whether it is stated on an organizational chart or earned through action, you are the person with authority. The authority to establish rules for appropriate behavior, reward appropriate behavior, and punish inappropriate behavior.

Second, you must always be identified with what is fair and just. There is no room for unjust, selfish, or self-serving behavior in any organization – large or small. Packer writes that, "an unjust judge . . . who has no interest in seeing right triumph over wrong, is . . . a monstrosity." An honest assessment of motivation and hidden agendas must always be in your mind. Remember the upward spiral?!?

Third, have the wisdom and the ability to discern truth in the actions of followers. Become able to determine factual truth as well as intent. Even more, be willing to speak those truths whenever and wherever they are encountered. Often, while paying a personal price to do so. Like me, coming down from 40,000 feet for followers when I'd much rather soar in solitude! People are usually defensive, even angry when forced to confront the inappropriateness of their behavior. We don't like to be "called out" or held accountable. Yet, an important aspect of knowing how to lead is being able to confront inappropriate behavior and gain a positive result. Remember DESC?!?

Last, you are the one with power. The power to carry out reward and punishment – not threaten. Be equally willing to enforce both.

Why this discussion about leaders as judges? What difference does it make? Wouldn't it "just happen" if you are a good leader?

No.

We are often surprised and disappointed when people we look up to get caught committing crimes or behaving unethically. Almost immediately, every beneficial thing she has ever done is re-examined for ulterior motives. Usually, her body of contributions is tossed out with the identified failure. That's insane! It's also a great example of the Halo Effect in action . . .

Unless she belongs to the scant percentage of the population who are truly sociopathic, she's just like the rest of us; a person trying to do what she feels is the only or best option in a given situation. Good people frequently do wrong things for, what they believe are, good reasons.

Our nature is such that we want to be liked, we want to be loved and accepted, we want to be praised and acclaimed. Although none of these wants are bad, they can become flaws in our ability when it comes to judgment. How many of us have watched a parent and child in a public place doing that dance, "We're in public and I don't want people to think I'm a bad parent?" You know the one. The child loudly asks for something he or she has already been told "no" about. The parent, reluctant to cause a scene in public and not wanting to appear to be a bad parent, gives in rather than sticking to and enforcing the standard.

You have to know your followers to be able to effectively, fairly, and wisely judge them. You must understand their motivations and goals. Otherwise, there is no just way for you to give them what they need based on their actions. Remember . . . walk in *their* shoes!

We tend to judge others by their actions and ourselves by our intent. In order to effectively judge our followers (and others), we must learn and understand their intent almost as well as our own, and render judgment – reward or punishment – accordingly.

Judgment is not based on capricious, self-indulgent, impulsive, or ignoble reaction to the activities or deeds of followers. Rather, it's based on the righteousness and justice, truth, and integrity that come from knowing our followers intent.

We must be both generous to and disciplining of followers.

Sound simple?

Seems obvious?

Because of our own characteristics and tendencies, those who are in positions or roles of authority frequently have a flawed view of their own role. All around us we see others who are generous, tolerant, open-minded and kind toward those who follow them. Likewise, we see those who are authoritative, firm, decisive, or forceful. Neither represents leadership in the absence of the other.

She must be able to give to followers in ways that are not selfish or self-seeking.

He gives, not just what the followers deserve or earn, but what they need to be successful. Likewise, he objectively and effectively determines that a follower is not productive and most important, why they aren't.

She must be able to respond with decisive, fair, and warranted discipline. Not a discipline borne of impatience or anger; but discipline that draws her follower away from being unproductive toward success; away from ineffectiveness toward achievement.

He must be willing to be loved, but not always liked and the followers must be willing to be led.

She has to see each follower as an individual, to discern strengths as well as shortcomings and the followers must be willing to acknowledge her insights.

He must be consistent and the followers must be responsive.

She must be fair and the followers have to appreciate what she has to offer.

He must be patient, responsive and trusting as the followers learn to be led and the followers must be objective in their assessment of him, realizing that he is still "human."

Without this balance of judgment and trust, neither the leader nor the follower can achieve the desired outcome. What is that outcome? . . . A successful, happy, and productive follower being led by someone who is loving, just, impartial, unbiased, inclusive, and responsive.

Leadership requires that we have authority over, affection and concern for, and an inclusive relationship with, our followers. It also requires that we put our followers in position to succeed and be recognized for their success.

Last Thoughts

In the last *Harry Potter* book by J. K. Rowling, Hermione had a tent that looked small and insignificant outside, but inside had all the comforts of home—everything that she, Harry, and Ron needed to be safe, warm and dry while in hiding. That's what makes people want to follow. Knowing that you will provide the location of and site number at the campground, give them a map to get there, and help them avoid obstacles or take advantage of opportunities they will encounter on the way. Believing that you will check in with them and not abandon them as they journey, adjusting their course when they get off track or the site number changes.

People will follow you when they know why they can trust you, that you won't change your mind and not tell them, or that you won't leave them hanging because you found a better location and it only had room for a few, not everyone. That's when people will follow you anywhere.

Confidence must be balanced with Humility and Justice must balance Mercy. Too much of either ultimately results in ineffective, unethical, or even immoral leadership.

Begin the way you plan to continue.

Don't start if you can't finish.

Ignorance is one thing. Stupidity can't be helped.

After the coronation, you'd better know what's next!

With the tone and facial expression that only a teenage female can master, I looked at my mother one day after she had corrected me about something . . . again. "You're not raising me like other mothers raise their daughters," I sneered. "It's like I'm being groomed or something."

Without missing a beat, The Princess Royal smiled at me and replied, "Of course you are. That's what you do with a princess in training."

My mouth hanging open in shock, Mommy kissed the top of my forehead, gently patted my cheek, and said, "Close your mouth, joyce. Ladies don't gape." After smiling again, she turned and walked away.

It wasn't until many years later that I realized what she had shown and taught me all my life. *What* you do isn't *nearly* as important as *Who* you are and *How* you interact with others. That's what makes you a leader worth following.

Gracias Mamacita . . .

About the Author

Entrepreneur, visionary, collaborative, exceptional communicator, critical thinker, and a leader's leader- just a few of the adjectives that have been used to describe Dr. joyce gillie gossom. With more than 35 years of professional experience in business and academics, joyce discovered her passion and purpose as a child – making a difference.

Born in Chicago, Illinois, joyce has spent her life going against the grain to make her difference. At the age of 16, she felt so connected to the poetry and style of e.e. cummings that her mother let joyce legally change her name to all lower case letters, which is frequently met with strong resistance.

Passionate about education, joyce began her career as a teacher and later obtained her masters in adult education and supervision and doctorate in curriculum and instruction. She has developed curriculum, taught, and been an Associate Dean at higher education institutions. She honed corporate, business, and entrepreneurial skills while managing leadership, training, and strategic planning organizations. joyce provided organizational and needs assessment consulting services to bring diverse groups and communities together to solve challenges. Graduates from her leadership development program went on to become elected government officials, major metropolitan school district superintendents and state college presidents. Currently, joyce serves as Executive Director for the National Association of Branch Campus Administrators and as a principal with Best Gurl inc, the unique, multi-platform company she operates with her husband. A highly sought out public speaker, joyce delivers powerful messages to businesses and associations.

Inspired by a small number of known and mostly unknown history makers, joyce strives to achieve, not by living up to the expectations of others, but by setting her own standards. A good description for her is the expression, "The one who follows the crowd will usually go no further than the crowd; those who walk alone are likely to find themselves in places no one has ever been before."

joyce and her husband have lived in Fort Walton Beach, Florida since 1999. She likes butterflies, the colors purple and yellow, Winnie the Pooh, and large bodies of water. You can reach her through BestGurl.com